Big Money
Is Looking For You

BISHOP DR. DEXTER JAMES

Dexter James Impartation Ministry
Email: thewealthambassador@hotmail.com
Telephone: 1-868-289-4325

All scripture quotations are taken from the King James Version of the Bible unless otherwise stated.

ISBN: 978-1-7328555-7-1

Printed in Trinidad and Tobago

My Personal Prayer for You.

This book is written to help the body of Christ remove the guilt of being rich or wanting to be rich or having a desire for good things. I will be showing you from the scriptures that good things are God things.

My prayer for you as you are about to read this book, is that the guilt or the concern of greed disappears from you, by your willingness and obedience to be generous to others as God will want you to be.

Say this prayer after me, "Father in the name of Jesus, open my eyes to your goodness, help me to fix my heart always on what you want from me from the abundance you have given to me, and I will give it. And I thank you for the opportunity you have given to me to enjoy the good things of this life in Jesus Mighty Name," Amen.

TABLE OF CONTENTS

CHAPTER ONE

Good Things are God Things

Child of God, you must know and always see God as a good God and Father who want you to have and enjoy good things. He also wants you to live good (holy and honest) and also to live well with others. If we get these two things right, living good (holy) and doing others good, we are major candidates for God to do good things for us.

In Genesis: 1:31, the Bible says, "And God saw everything that he had made, and, behold, it was very good." Now please note that everything God made was very good. Which means God is the originator of all good things. Good things are not the devil things, they are God things. What the devil does is take good things and influence people to pervert it and use it outside of God's original intent. For example, a woman was made for man, not another woman, but the enemy has perverted that. A man is supposed to have a woman as a wife, not another man yet the enemy perverted it. Money was supposed to be used as a form of exchange for goods and services but people use it to manipulate others, promote evil and many other diverted purposes. So many people have been turned off from good things or desiring good things because they have mostly seen the perverted side of those good things. But good things are God things.

In James: 1:17, the Bible says, "Every good and perfect gift is from above, and cometh down from the Father of lights, with who is no variableness, neither shadow of turning." So we see that when it is good and perfect (not perverted) it is of God, it came from above. The philosophy of good things and nice things is not a carnal philosophy, it is a heavenly philosophy, and it is an ordained philosophy. That is why the Bible told us to think on those things that are of good report. It is telling us to think on those scriptures that have reported good things about God. Also the scriptures in James tell us, God is not going to turn out to be bad or start doing bad things to good people.

I want you to know that good things have already left heaven for you. All you need to do is locate them through the scriptures by faith, so you will know what they are, and obtain them through your consistent believing and trusting in the word of God that cannot fail.

Psalms: 119:68, says "Thou (God) are good, and doest good; teach me thy statutes (laws)." The psalmist David is telling God, you are good and do good things, teach me your laws. Why would David be asking that? He is asking that because he wants to know how to experience the goodness of a good God. It is sad that so many believers who are walking in the fear (reverence) of the Lord are afraid of the goodness of a good God. It is possible to be saved, and not safe or secure where the goodness of God is, concerning your health, wealth, peace and personal safety if you are not taught right or refuse to believe right. All the promises of God work by faith that is why hearing what God says in His word is so important. You will always settle for less, when you refuse to believe that God wants you to have the best.

Saints, God wants you to know you are blessed so that you can enjoy the best.

Good things are God things, in Genesis: 2:12, this is what the Bible says about the gold in the land (Garden of Eden). “And the gold of that land is good.”

God created the universe to reflect Him; here is what the psalmist David says in Psalms: 33:5, “The earth is full of the goodness of the Lord.” That means the earth is loaded with the goodness of God. Moreover there are good things all over the earth, which also means all over the earth you can see a reflection of God when we come across anything that is good and perfect.

When the Bible says in Isaiah 52:7 NLT, "How beautiful on the mountains are the feet of the messenger who brings good news, the (God news) of peace and salvation, the news that the God of Israel reigns?" The gospel which is good news must be proclaimed, we must tell people that God is a good God, and He has done and is doing good things for you and I.

Firstly, He created a planet with everything we need for food, clothing and shelter. Secondly, He sent Jesus Christ to die in our place for our sins. Thirdly, He allowed Jesus to take thirty nine stripes for our healing. He allowed Jesus to be chastised for our peace. And lastly, He allowed Jesus to become poor that we might become rich through His poverty. This is the gospel; this is the good news that must be proclaimed to the masses worldwide uncompromisingly. Remember, the gospel is God's written acts (what He has already done) that He wants us to proclaim so people can hear it, believe it and then experience it. So the people can see His written acts in action (demonstration, enforcement, manifestation).

SAY THIS SEVEN TIMES

Good things are God things

Good things are God things

Good things are God things

Good things are God things

Good things are God things

Good things are God things

Good things are God things

I need you to say this for the next seven days, seven times, until this gets a hold of you and transforms you.

CHAPTER TWO

God Wants You To Enjoy and Experience Good Things

In this chapter, I am going to show you what the Bible has to say about God's desire for you to have the best and enjoy the best. Saints, after being born again, God has given us His word to stimulate the kind of desires He wants us to have that we can develop the faith that is necessary to acquire all the good things He has given to us, while we remain connected to Him. The caution in the Bible is never not having, it is giving Him first priority at all times, and not forgetting Him when things get good. So the caution was a *first place* caution, not a *having material things* caution. It was having material things and forgetting the main thing, the main one who gave material things.

Let us see what Paul told Timothy about this in 1 Timothy 6:17 , "Charge them that are rich in this world, that they be not high minded, nor trust in uncertain riches, but in the living God, who giveth us richly all things to enjoy." Paul told Timothy tell them do not trust riches; trust in the living God who give them richly all things to enjoy. Saints, all good things are God things for His people to enjoy. It is not for us to be destroyed or for us to destroy it, but was designed by God for us to enjoy it (good things).

It is God's desire and will for us to enjoy all the good and perfect things that He has created for us. That is why Psalms: 35:27 says that He (God) has pleasure in prosperity (success, increase, multiplication, blessings, and well-being) of His servants. When we are experiencing success and good things, it pleasures God because it says we are mature and walking in what He has desired for us.

Isaiah: 1:19 has this too; "If ye are willing and obedient, you shall eat the good of the land.
The good God of heaven says, if you meet my condition of being willing and obedient to my word, I am going to permit you to experience good in the land, even when things does not seem to be good in the land. God is also saying here, you are sustained by your obedience to Him, not by the state of the economy in your country or by the world's economy. Come on child of God, repeat this confession. "I shall eat good, because I am obedient to a good God. Say it again, I shall eat good, because I am obedient to a good God."

You have to believe it child of God, that your heavenly Father, God wants you to experience that which is good only.

In Deuteronomy: 8:7 the Bible said this, "For the Lord your God bringeth thee into a good land." This scripture says that God shall bring them into a good land. You know what kind of experience you will have in a good land? Good experience. God wants you to enter a place in your life where you are experiencing good things everyday of your life. It is a place that I call restful and stress less prosperity. That is God's desire for you child of God, a good land, a good business, good family life, good health, good career and good (sound) mind.

The Bible says in 2 Peter: 1:3; "According as His divine power hath given unto us all things that pertain to life and godliness." God has surely given us all things, not some things, all things, pertaining to life and godliness. That means I have everything that is required for a successful physical, financial and spiritual life. I am failure proof, because the good God of heaven has become my roof (covering, shield).

God got a lot of good things for you to enjoy if you will just obey Him. In Job 36:11, "If they obey and serve Him (God), they shall spend their days in prosperity, and their years in pleasures." That is what God wants you to experience. Nothing else is this good God's desire. He wants you to have it. Now if you look at His order, do Me right, and I will make right things start happening to you, right away.

God wants you to have that which is good; God wants you to experience that which is good. Look at Psalms 84:11, "For the Lord is a sun and shield: the Lord will give grace and glory: no good thing will he withhold from them that walk uprightly." God is not withholding good things from us; He has been holding good things for us. Give God a life that is pleasing to Him, and He will give you a life that is pleasing to you and Him.

I want you to make this confession twelve times, and then do it at least once for the next twelve days, everyday. Meditate on this strongly as you say it. You may ask why Apostle or Bishop? Because I am trying to get you to reprogrammed your mindset, and get it set for good things.

God wants me to experience and enjoy good things, because they are His things.
God wants me to experience and enjoy good things, because they are His things.
God wants me to experience and enjoy good things, because they are His thing.
God wants me to experience and enjoy good things, because they are His things.
God wants me to experience and enjoy good things, because they are His things.
God wants me to experience and enjoy good things, because they are His things.

God wants me to experience and enjoy good things, because they are His things.
God wants me to experience and enjoy good things, because they are His things.
God wants me to experience and enjoy good things, because they are His things.
God wants me to experience and enjoy good thing, because they are His things.
God wants me to experience and enjoy good things, because they are His things.
God wants me to experience and enjoy good things, because they are His things.

It is your turn to experience good things, and enjoy it permanently.

CHAPTER THREE

God Does Good Things

God is a good God and He does good things. We have to see God as the author of that which is good and see the devil as the author of that which is bad. Because God is good, He does good things over and over and over and over again. All He requires of His people is just to do good and behave good so that they can experience the good things He has already prepared for them.

This is what the Bible say in Ephesians 2:10 NKJV, "For we are His (God) workmanship, created in Christ Jesus for good works, which God prepared beforehand that we should walk in them. God has prepared good works for us to walk in, not bad works, not just works, the Bible say good works. This means the God that is good wants us to have that which is good and want us to experience that which is good. That means God only has planned good works for us because the good God does good always.

God's good plans for us are also confirmed in Jeremiah 29:11 NLT Bible, "For I know plans I have for you, says the Lord." They are plans for good and not for disaster, to give you a future and a hope. So God planned out our lives for good and not evil, not failure. When God planned out our lives He said they will go through bad stuff, but it has to end well, because I have planned it good, it has to end just like how I planned it from the beginning. That is why Romans 8:28 says, "And we know that all things work together for good to them that love God, to them who are called according to His purpose."

It has to work for good, because God planned your life well. God only wants you to experience and enjoy that which is good.

In life you will experience bad and difficult situations, but that must never bring you to a place of hopelessness. It must bring you to a place of greater God consciousness and awareness about His plan and purpose for your life. A bad situation does not necessarily mean a bad life. There are many people lives that started bad in the Bible but ended up good, you remember Joseph and David, hated by their brothers, over looked by their fathers, but loved by God. And their lives ended well, because God's good plan that He has planned in advance for their lives came to pass. In due season, God will bring all things into alignment when you believe and the time is right.

I love this, Psalms 119:68 says in the WEB translation "You (God) are good, and do good." Saints, God is a good God and Father and He does good things for all of His Children, especially for the ones who please Him. He says this to them that please Him in Psalms 84:11, "No good thing will He withhold from them that walk uprightly." If you walk upright, God will do you right.

God sent Jesus to earth to mirror His mind, will and intent for mankind. That is why the Bible says in Acts 10:38, "How God anointed Jesus of Nazareth with the Holy Ghost and with power who went about doing good, and healing all that were oppressed of the devil for God was with Him." Now we see God was with Jesus using Him to do good. Child of God your poverty, your lack, your insufficiency, your needs, your debts have come up before God, and He is saying to you, will you believe me to do something good for you? It is not if it can be done, it is not if God can do it, it is if you can believe Him to do it. God does good things and He wants you to experience something good and good things all the days of your life.

The Bible says in Joshua 21:45 ESV, "Not a one word of all the good promises that the Lord had made to the house of Israel had failed; all came to pass." Please note His good promises. God only makes good promises to His beloved. So we see He promised good things because He wants us to believe for good things.

Repeat this confession for me three times and do it after for three days, three times a day until it soaks inside of your spirit.

God does Good things, and He has done good things for me

God does good things, and He has done good things for me

God does good things, and He has done good things for me

CHAPTER FOUR

God Wants To Take Care of You

God wants to take care of you is a statement that most people ignore until they really cannot do anything for themselves. God will take care of you does not mean being lazy, careless or reckless. What it means is trusting God to take care of you fully that your income does not determine the outcome of your life but your faith in God to provide for you determines that.

Psalms 78:19 says in the NLT Bible, “They spoke against God himself, saying, God can’t give us food in the wilderness.” This got God angry because they placed a limit on His ability to take care of them. Child of God, it does not matter where you are or what is happening to the economy negatively in your country, God promised to take care of you and it is still a sure thing.

Trusting God to take care of you has to be a relationship thing. You have to grow in your relationship with God over a period of time and consistently rely on Him, when others, the devil and even your mind try to tell you a lie about Him, to make you think He will not come through and He will fail you. It is only your relationship with God will determine your level of trust you have in Him. God will prepare a table before you in the presence of your enemies; you will be eating up, while they are beating up or fighting up.

Paul made the statement in Philippians 4:19, when he said "my God shall supply all your needs." He was not saying God will take care of some of your needs, he said my God will shall supply all your needs. The same God that Paul is talking about who supplies all His needs is the same God that will supply your needs.

The psalmist David said in Psalms 23:1, "The Lord is my Shepherd, I shall not want. There are other translations which say it this way, "The Lord is my Shepherd (NIV I lack nothing, NLT I have all I need, ESV I shall not want, CEV, I will never be in need, GNT, I have everything I need)." There is a way to say this, if I have God, it is all I need to eliminate all of my needs.

The first thing one must do is to develop a scriptural relationship with God and always put the things of God first. God is not obligated to take care of selfish people. He is only obligated to take care of those who have given themselves to Him fully. In Matthew 6:33, the Bible says, seek ye first the kingdom of God and His righteousness and then all these other (material) things shall be added unto you. If you do the seeking, God will do the adding.

The children of Israel were sustained for forty years with no supermarket in the wilderness, and if you are not in a wilderness why are you afraid of God not coming through for you. God wants to take care of you. The Bible said in Psalms 34:10, "but they who seek the Lord shall not want any good thing." You shall not lack anything good, if you keep seeking the good God. You will not lack anything good, if you and God stay good.

Jesus sent out His disciples with no money and nothing to sustain themselves because He wanted to sustain them. This is what He eventually asked them when they returned in Luke 22:35, NLT, "Then Jesus asked them, when I sent you out to preach the good news and you did not have money, a traveller's bag, or an extra pair of sandals, did you need anything? No, they replied." You can never run out, when you serve a running over God. If God sent you out, you will never have to go without or do without.

CHAPTER FIVE

Big Money is Looking for You

Big money is looking for you. It is waiting on you, it wants to locate you. Your righteousness is your qualifier; your obedience to God positions you to have the wealth of the wicked. This is not the wealth you work for, this is the one the wicked work for, and have piled up, laid up, heaped up, stored up which God said they were doing it for you. What is sad, most believers don't even know that God has given sinners and wicked people a ministry of gathering wealth for the righteous. The righteous do not work for wealth, the righteous obey for wealth. Do what God tell you to do and then trust Him to take care of you. Trust Him to supply all that you will need, want and desire.

Proverbs 13:22 in the AMPC translation says, "And the wealth of the sinner [finds its way eventually] into the hands of the righteous, for whom it was laid up. This scripture tells you and I who are righteous, that we are beneficiaries of all sinners' wealth. We are inheritors of what they have laid up. That mean we just need to state our claim, so what is laid up, can locate us.

The Bible says, it eventually finds its way, that means it does not matter who is messing with what have been already declare ours, it is coming to us. It does not matter who is holding on to what is ours, they have to let it go because we are the rightful owners. This scripture lets us know we do not have to look for money or pursue money, we just have to obey, what God said and the money will locate us, the land will locate us, the house will locate us, the car will locate us. The Bible also said that it will eventually find us, which means it has been looking for us. Big money, large money, huge money is looking for us (the righteous, those who are in right standing with God).

The Bible never promotes working for money to live for believers which is the world system. God's systems, the kingdom system is obeying Godly instructions, live, prosper and have good success. Our prosperity is laid up, so we never have to work for it, other people did that, what we have to do is obey for it. And this is confirmed in Deuteronomy 28, the first few verses; it keeps saying "If you obey my commandments or my law, all these Blessings will come upon you."

Isaiah chapter 1:19 says, "If we are willing and obedient we will eat the good of the land." Job 36:11, says, "If they obey and serve Him they will spend their days in prosperity and their years in pleasure." So over and over again in the scriptures we are seeing that the key to walking in the God kind of prosperity is not work, it is obedience. There are so many ways God can use to bless us beyond what we can think or even ask. But believers have limited God's supply to work, business, lack of employment or education. Child of God the blessings of God do not discriminate, it works with whoever believes, if you believe God will do it, He will. If you doubt it, you will live without it. If you have faith for it, then you will surely experience it, in Jesus mighty name.

The Bible says in Deuteronomy: 28:2, "That blessings will overtake us, that means it has been looking for us, and when it find us, it spreads all around us and ahead of us." There is a real grace and anointing for supernatural supply, but you have to really, really believe it, you have to know about it, you have to trust God fully to walk in it. It is only God who can supply this fully.

Luke: 6:38 NLT says, "Give, and you will receive. Your gift will return to you in full -pressed down, shaken together to make room for more, running over, and poured into your lap." That means after you give, big money is looking for you, to surprise you, to overload you. Child of God giving to God is good, but it is not good enough to walk in the overflow, you have to believe that God will do His part that He has promised, just like He has promised.

Prayer for Salvation and against Greed

Repeat this prayer after me if you do not know Jesus as your Lord and Saviour. "Father I ask you to forgive me of my sins, come into my heart and save me. I believe with my heart and confess with my mouth that Jesus died for my sins, He shed His blood and was buried and on the third day he arose. Thank you for saving me."

Now my next prayer is against greed.

"Father I thank you for delivering and setting me free from all known and unknown selfishness in my life. May I never be a hoarder, let me be a spirit led giver. And let me never be ashamed of walking in abundance as a good steward in Jesus Might Name Amen."

Thank you for reading this book.

May you look out for that which has been looking for you in Jesus Name Amen.

Big Money is Looking for You.

Should you believe God is leading you to ***Warriors Assembly Growing Church Breakthrough Ministries***, here are our current locations:

1. Princes Town (Restoration City)

Bless Avenue, New Grant, Princess Town

1 (868) 347-7180, 494-4604

2. Couva (Head Quarters)

147 Southern Main Road

1 (868) 289-4325, 388-2769

3. Aripero (House of Prophetic Destiny)

1414 Aripero Village, Rousillac

(Deo's Shopping Mall) 1 (868) 752-0056

4. Siparia (House of Power)

15 High Street (Upstairs KFC)

1 (868) 491-7153

5. Arouca (House of Uncommon Wisdom)

11 Eastern Main Road, (Upstairs BJ's Drug World)

Five Rivers 1 (868) 289-4325

***Chaguanas (Winner's Chapel)**

2nd Floor, Regency Business Centre

Cnr Penco & Gaston Streets

1 (868) 289-4325

Made in United States
North Haven, CT
04 November 2026

21767739R00021